Contents

Have you eaten green foods?

Colours are all around you.

How many different colours can you see in these foods?

All of these foods are green.

Which ones have you eaten?

What are some green fruits?

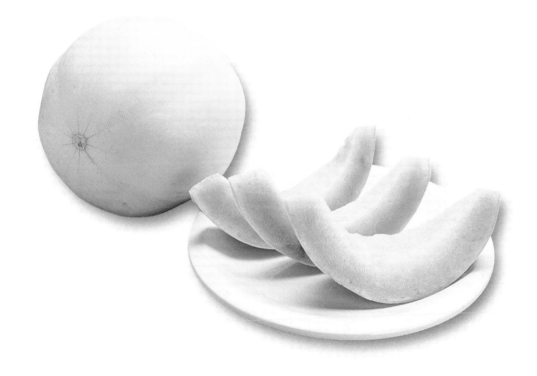

Some melons are big and green.

Honeydew melons are sweet
and juicy.

Watermelons are sweet and juicy, too!

The hard green skin of a watermelon is called the **rind**.

7

What are some green vegetables?

These cabbages have dark green **leaves**.

Cabbages are good for you.

Lettuce leaves are green, too.

We eat them in **salads**.

Have you tried these juicy green fruits?

Some grapes are green.

Grapes grow on **vines**.

Limes have shiny green skin.

They grow on trees.

Have you tried these green vegetables?

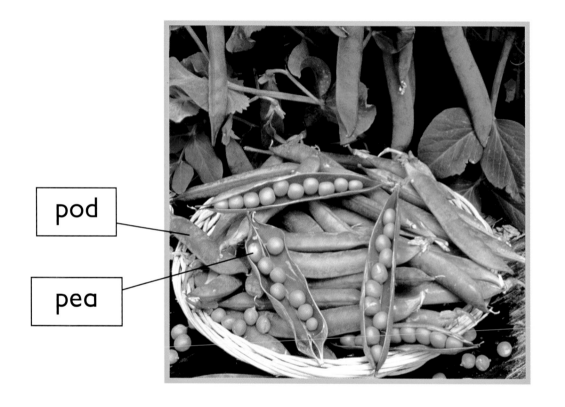

pod

pea

Peas are green and good for you.

They grow inside **pods**.

Brussels sprouts are good for you, too.

They look like little cabbages!

What green parts of plants do we eat?

We eat the **stem** of the celery plant.

Celery is crunchy and is good in **salads**.

We eat the flowers of the broccoli plant.

Broccoli is good for you, too.

Have you tried these soft green fruits?

Kiwi fruit have lots of **seeds** in them.

They are tasty in fruit **salad**.

The inside of an avocado is soft and green.

Sometimes people eat mashed avocados.

What soups and drinks are green?

Pea soup is made by cooking dried peas.

Add fresh peas to make it bright green!

Limeade is a green drink.

It is made by squeezing the juice out of limes.

Recipe: Crunchy Green Salad

! Ask an adult to help you.

First, wash some lettuce, celery and cucumber.

Next, cut them into small pieces.

Then, mix the vegetables in a bowl.

Now, eat your crunchy green **salad**!

Quiz

Can you name these green foods?

Look for the answers on page 24.

Glossary

leaves
the flat parts attached to the stem of a plant

pod
case that some beans and peas grow in

rind
hard skin on the outside of a fruit or vegetable

salad
a cold dish made up of chopped fruit or vegetables

seed
the part of a plant that grows into another plant

stem
the main part of a plant which grows from the ground

vine
a plant that has a very long, thin stem

Index

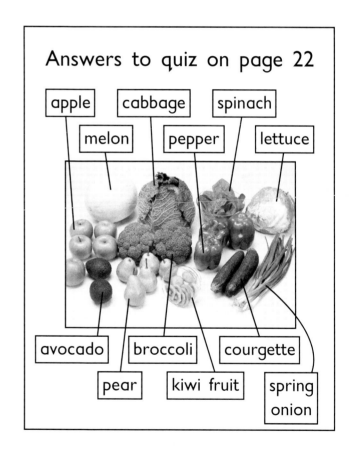

Answers to quiz on page 22

apple   cabbage   spinach

melon   pepper   lettuce

avocado   broccoli   courgette

pear   kiwi fruit   spring onion